THE KANSAS CITY CHIEFS

BY

MARK STEWART

Content Consultant
Jason Aikens

HA CASS COUNTY PUBLIC LIBRARY
400 E. MECHANIC
HARRISONVILLE, MO 64701

NORWOODHOUSE PRESS
CHICAGO, ILLINOIS

Norwood House Press
P.O. Box 316598
Chicago, Illinois 60631

For information regarding Norwood House Press, please visit our website at:
www.norwoodhousepress.com or call 866-565-2900.

PHOTO CREDITS:
All photos courtesy of Getty Images except the following:
Topps, Inc. (6, 14, 16, 20, 21, 28, 29, 30, 34 right, 35 top & bottom left
& top right, 37, 38, 40 all, 41 top & bottom right, 43);
Black Book Partners Archives (9, 22, 36, 39, 41 left);
Author's Collection (34 left); Matt Richman (48 top).
Cover photo: David Drapkin/Getty Images
Special thanks to Topps, Inc.

Editor: Mike Kennedy
Designer: Ron Jaffe
Project Management: Black Book Partners, LLC.
Research: Evan Frankel
Special thanks to: Ian Guerin

LIBRARY OF CONGRESS CATALOGING-IN-PUBLICATION DATA

Stewart, Mark, 1960-
  The Kansas City Chiefs / by Mark Stewart ; content consultant Jason
Aikens.
    p. cm. -- (Team spirit)
  Includes bibliographical references and index.
  Summary: "Presents the history, accomplishments and key personalities of
the Kansas City Chiefs football team. Includes timelines, quotes, maps,
glossary and websites"--Provided by publisher.
  ISBN-13: 978-1-59953-208-0 (library edition : alk. paper)
  ISBN-10: 1-59953-208-5 (library edition : alk. paper) 1. Kansas City
Chiefs (Football team)--History--Juvenile literature. I. Aikens, Jason. II.
Title.
  GV956.K35S84 2008
  796.332'6409778411--dc22
                                                    2008012741

COVER PHOTO: The Chiefs huddle during a 2006 game to call a play on offense.

Table of Contents

SPORTS WORDS & VOCABULARY WORDS: In this book, you will find many words that are new to you. You may also see familiar words used in new ways. The glossary on page 46 gives the meanings of football words, as well as "everyday" words that have special football meanings. These words appear in **bold type** throughout the book. The glossary on page 47 gives the meanings of vocabulary words that are not related to football. They appear in ***bold italic type*** throughout the book.

Meet the Chiefs

When someone is "seeing red," it means they are angry. When football fans in Kansas City see red, they couldn't be happier. Since the 1960s, the Chiefs have been one of the most popular teams in football. During that time, few sports teams have ever had a closer bond with their fans.

The Chiefs love to find record-smashing superstars and combine them with rock-solid players who know how to run, throw, **block**, and tackle. When the Kansas City players have the fans behind them, they are almost impossible to beat.

This book tells the story of the Chiefs. They started as the "dream come true" of a great American sportsman. They later helped make **professional** football the popular game it is today. When a Kansas City player pulls on his helmet and runs out to the field, he becomes part of a great *tradition*.

Larry Johnson is congratulated by happy teammates after scoring a touchdown during a 2007 game.

Way Back When

Texas millionaire Lamar Hunt was used to getting what he wanted. There was one thing that he could *not* get—a team in the **National Football League (NFL)**. Tired of trying, Hunt helped start the **American Football League (AFL)**. He owned the Dallas Texans, who played their first game in 1960—the same year the NFL's Dallas Cowboys started.

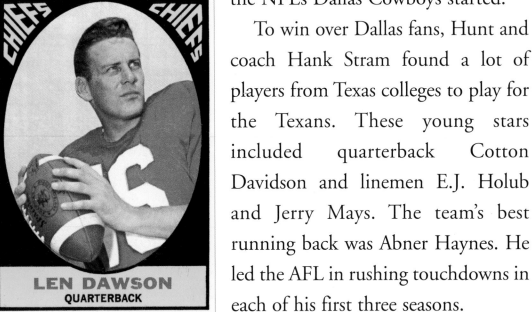

LEN DAWSON
QUARTERBACK

To win over Dallas fans, Hunt and coach Hank Stram found a lot of players from Texas colleges to play for the Texans. These young stars included quarterback Cotton Davidson and linemen E.J. Holub and Jerry Mays. The team's best running back was Abner Haynes. He led the AFL in rushing touchdowns in each of his first three seasons.

In 1962, the Texans signed quarterback Len Dawson. He led Dallas to the **AFL Championship**. Other stars on that team included Jim Tyrer, Fred Arbanas, Chris Burford, Bobby Hunt, and

Johnny Robinson. A few months after their victory, the Texans moved to Kansas City, Missouri and became the Chiefs. Hunt no longer wanted to compete with the Cowboys, and Kansas City fans were hungry for a new team.

The AFL and NFL joined forces in 1970. During the AFL's ten years, the Chiefs had the best record of any team: 87 wins, 48 losses, and five ties. They won two more AFL Championships, in 1966 and 1969. The Chiefs played in the first **Super Bowl** in 1967 and lost to the Green Bay Packers. They returned to the Super Bowl three years later and beat the Minnesota Vikings.

Kansas City had a well-balanced team during the 1960s. Running back Mike Garrett and receiver Otis Taylor starred with Dawson on offense. The defense was led by Buck Buchanan, Bobby Bell, Willie Lanier, and Emmitt Thomas. Jan Stenerud was the team's kicker.

In the NFL, the Chiefs played in the competitive **Western Division** of the **American Football Conference (AFC)**. During the 1970s and 1980s, they struggled to finish ahead of the Oakland

Raiders, Denver Broncos, and San Diego Chargers. Kansas City fans still had some exciting players to root for, including receivers Stephon Paige and Carlos Carlson, quarterbacks Bill Kenney and Steve DeBerg, running back Christian Okoye, and defensive stars Art Still, Deron Cherry, and Albert Lewis.

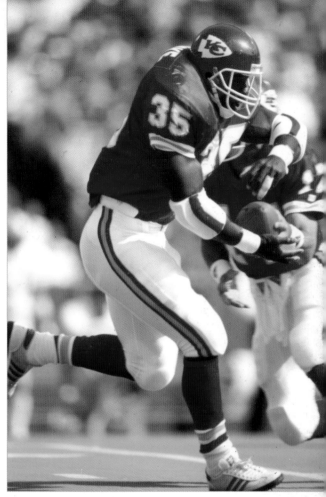

In the early 1990s, the Chiefs returned to their winning ways. They were led by two NFL legends, Joe Montana and Marcus Allen. Young pass rushers Neil Smith and Derrick Thomas turned Kansas City's defense into one of the toughest in the league. The Chiefs made it all the way to the 1993 **AFC Championship** game. Smith and Thomas carried the team to two more **AFC West** championships in the 1990s, but a third trip to the Super Bowl was just beyond their grasp. The Chiefs and their fans began the 21st *century* with high hopes and great expectations.

LEFT: Derrick Thomas, who led the Chiefs back to the top of the AFC in the 1990s.   **ABOVE**: Christian Okoye takes a handoff.

The Team Today

Since 2000, the Chiefs have been one of the most entertaining teams in the AFC. Kansas City fans have been treated to great performances by running backs Priest Holmes, Tony Richardson, and Larry Johnson, receivers Tony Gonzalez and Dwayne Bowe, quarterback Trent Green, and super-fast kick returner Dante Hall.

The days when a football team could keep all of its players together for ten years—as the Chiefs did in the 1960s and 1970s—are over. Kansas City has changed its *strategy* to work in today's NFL. Each year, the Chiefs build their team around a small *core* of leaders. They **draft** young players, sign **free agents**, and trade for experienced stars.

Some things will never change about Chiefs football. Their fans will always be among the loudest in sports. The energy in the stadium will always give the players a great advantage. And Kansas City will always have at least one special player who will take your breath away.

Tony Gonzalez celebrates with teammates after a touchdown during a 2007 game.

First National Bank
CHIEFS
Nationwide
On Your Side
GATES
BAR-B-Q
AVAILABLE AT
SECTIONS 112 & 131,
GATE B & F SPIRALS
SECTIONS 324 & 346
PRICE CHOPPER
3 JAN STENERUD 1967-79
42 JOHNNY ROBINSON 1960-71
TOSHIBA
COPY • FAX • PRINT
CHIEFS 3 T.O.L. 3 7:05 T.O.L. 3 BENGALS
QTR 1 DOWN 2 TO GO 10 BALL ON 12
L. JOHNSON
McINTOSH

Home Turf

During their three seasons in Dallas, the Texans played in the Cotton Bowl. It was one of the most famous stadiums in football. After the team moved to Kansas City, the Chiefs made their new home in Municipal Stadium. At one point, it was used by a legendary African-American baseball team called the Monarchs. The Chiefs first shared Municipal Stadium with the Kansas City Athletics baseball team and later with the Kansas City Royals baseball team.

In 1972, the Chiefs moved to brand-new Arrowhead Stadium. They played on *artificial* turf until 1994, when the team changed to a natural grass field. In 2007, the Chiefs announced that they would spend $375 million to *modernize* Arrowhead Stadium. The "new" Arrowhead should be done by 2011.

BY THE NUMBERS

- *Arrowhead Stadium has 79,451 seats for football.*
- *The Chiefs beat the New Orleans Saints 20–17 in the first regular-season game played in their stadium.*
- *In 1972, a record 82,094 fans squeezed into Arrowhead for a game between the Chiefs and Oakland Raiders.*

Fans in Arrowhead Stadium watch as the Chiefs run a play on offense.

Dressed for Success

Most football fans believe that the name "Chiefs" was inspired by Native American leaders. Although the team honors this great *heritage*, the name actually came from the mayor of Kansas City during the 1960s. H. Roe Bartle made the team a generous offer to move from Dallas in 1963, and owner Lamar Hunt chose the new name as a thank you. Bartle was a leader of the Boy Scouts of America, and everyone called him the "Chief."

Bobby Bell models the team's uniform from the 1960s.

When the Texans played in Dallas, their uniform colors were red, white, and gold. When the team moved to Kansas City, Hunt kept the same colors. The Chiefs still use them today.

The Chiefs have used the same helmet design since 1963. It is a white arrowhead on a red helmet, with the letters *KC* written in red. The team jerseys have always used a combination of red and white. The color gold has usually been featured in stripes on the pants, sleeves, and socks.

UNIFORM BASICS

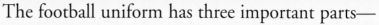

The football uniform has three important parts—

- Helmet
- Jersey
- Pants

Helmets used to be made out of leather, and they did not have facemasks—ouch! Today, helmets are made of super-strong plastic. The uniform top, or jersey, is made of thick fabric. It fits snugly around a player so that tacklers cannot grab it and pull him down. The pants come down just over the knees.

There is a lot more to a football uniform than what you see on the outside. Air can be pumped inside the helmet to give it a snug, padded fit. The jersey covers shoulder pads, and sometimes a rib protector called a flak jacket. The pants include pads that protect the hips, thighs, *tailbone*, and knees.

Football teams have two sets of uniforms— one dark and one light. This makes it easier to tell two teams apart on the field. Almost all teams wear their dark uniforms at home and their light ones on the road.

Dwayne Bowe lines up wearing the team's home uniform during a 2007 game.

We Won!

From 1962 to 1970, the Chiefs won three AFL Championships and one Super Bowl. The team's first championship came in its final season as the Dallas Texans. The other titles came as the Kansas City Chiefs.

The 1962 Texans were led by Len Dawson, Jim Tyrer, Fred Arbanas, and Johnny Robinson. All four stars would remain with the team through its next three championships. In their first AFL title game, the Texans played the Houston Oilers. Abner Haynes scored two touchdowns in the first half to help Dallas to a 17–0 lead.

In the second half, the Oilers came back. They scored a touchdown with five minutes left in the fourth quarter, and the game went into **overtime**. Neither team scored in the first 15-minute period. Finally, Dallas's Tommy Brooker kicked a field goal to end the longest game in pro football history. The Texans celebrated their first championship ever.

The Chiefs took the AFL crown again in 1966. This time, they played the Buffalo Bills in the championship game. The winner would face the NFL champions in the first Super Bowl. The Chiefs had added more good players to their **lineup**, including receiver Otis Taylor, running back Mike Garrett, and defensive stars Buck Buchanan, Bobby Bell, Jerry Mays, Emmitt Thomas, and Fred Williamson.

Against the Bills, the offense and defense both were *dominant*. Dawson connected with Arbanas and Taylor for touchdowns, and Garrett scored twice on runs. The Bills could do nothing when they

LEFT: Jim Tyrer, the leader of Kansas City's offensive line in the 1960s.
ABOVE: Len Dawson hands off to Mike Garrett in the 1966 AFL Championship.

had the ball, and the Chiefs won 31–7. Two weeks later, Kansas City played the Green Bay Packers in Super Bowl I. The Chiefs lost 35–10.

Kansas City was determined to get back to the big game and win it. In 1969, the Chiefs defeated the New York Jets in the **playoffs**, and then faced their greatest *rivals*, the Oakland Raiders, in the last AFL Championship game. The Raiders had won both of their regular-season meetings, but this time the Chiefs came out on top. Their pass rush was unstoppable. Kansas City won 17–7.

The Chiefs faced the Minnesota Vikings in Super Bowl IV. The Vikings were a scary team. They wore down defenses with their tough runners and gobbled up quarterbacks with their defensive line. The Chiefs had one big advantage— they had been to the Super Bowl before.

Kansas City's players weren't nervous and quickly got down to business.

The Chiefs confused the Minnesota defense with their running plays. They also did a great job blocking pass rushers Jim Marshall and Carl Eller. Dawson had all the extra time he needed to find open receivers. Jan Stenerud kicked three field goals, and the Chiefs scored two touchdowns to win 23–7. In Kansas City's tenth season, the team stood atop the pro football world.

LEFT: The Chiefs stop the New York Jets on a running play. Kansas City played excellent team defense.   **ABOVE**: The Chiefs carry Hank Stram off the field after their win in Super Bowl IV.

Go-To Guys

To be a true star in the NFL, you need more than fast feet and a big body. You have to be a "go-to guy"—someone the coach wants on the field at the end of a big game. Fans of the Texans and Chiefs have had a lot to cheer about over the years, including these great stars …

THE PIONEERS

LEN DAWSON   Quarterback

• BORN: 6/20/1935   • PLAYED FOR TEAM: 1962 TO 1975

Few quarterbacks have ever thrown the ball with more *poise* or accuracy than Len Dawson. He rarely made a bad pass and never *panicked* when the Chiefs were trailing. In 1962, Dawson teamed up with his old college coach, Hank Stram, to win the AFL Championship.

No. 15 in a series of 16   QT.C.G.—PRTD. IN U.S.A.

BOBBY BELL   Linebacker

• BORN: 6/17/1940   • PLAYED FOR TEAM: 1963 TO 1974

Bobby Bell probably could have played any position on the field. He was **All-AFL** as a defensive end in 1964 and All-AFL as a linebacker in 1965. Bell used his quick hands and feet as well as any linebacker who ever played.

BUCK BUCHANAN   Defensive Lineman

- BORN: 9/10/1940   • PLAYED FOR TEAM: 1963 TO 1975

Buck Buchanan was the top pick in the 1963 AFL draft. He was fast enough to tackle runners along the sidelines and tall enough to knock down passes that others could not reach. Buchanan was voted **All-Pro** four times.

OTIS TAYLOR   Receiver

- BORN: 8/11/1942   • PLAYED FOR TEAM: 1965 TO 1975

Otis Taylor had long strides and great speed. Many defensive backs thought they had him covered, only to watch him shift into a higher gear and run past them. Taylor led the NFL in receiving yards in 1971.

JAN STENERUD   Kicker

- BORN: 11/26/1942   • PLAYED FOR TEAM: 1967 TO 1979

Jan Stenerud was the most successful of the early **soccer-style** kickers. He led the AFL in field goals as a **rookie**. In 1991, Stenerud became the first full-time kicker to join the **Hall of Fame**.

MIDDLE LINEBACKER
WILLIE LANIER

WILLIE LANIER   Linebacker

- BORN: 8/21/1945   • PLAYED FOR TEAM: 1967 TO 1977

Willie Lanier was a hard tackler and good pass defender. He was the first African-American to star at middle linebacker. Many believed that Lanier was the best **all-around** player at his position during the 1970s.

LEFT: Len Dawson
RIGHT: Willie Lanier

MODERN STARS

NEIL SMITH   Defensive Lineman

- BORN: 4/10/1966   • PLAYED FOR TEAM: 1988 TO 1996

Neil Smith played defensive end opposite Derrick Thomas. This gave the Chiefs All-Pro pass rushers on both sides of the field. Smith led the NFL in **sacks** in 1993. He made the **Pro Bowl** six times.

DERRICK THOMAS   Linebacker

- BORN: 1/1/1967   • DIED: 2/8/2000
- PLAYED FOR TEAM: 1989 TO 1999

Derrick Thomas terrified quarterbacks. He was too big and fast for one player to block, and opponents never knew when or where he would burst across the line. In his second season, Thomas led the NFL with 20 sacks.

WILL SHIELDS Offensive Lineman

- BORN: 9/15/1971
- PLAYED FOR TEAM: 1993 TO 2006

Will Shields ruled the line from his position at right guard. He was an excellent run blocker and even better at protecting the quarterback on passing plays. Shields was a Pro Bowler 12 years in a row.

TONY GONZALEZ   Tight End

• BORN: 2/27/1976   • FIRST SEASON WITH TEAM: 1997

Tony Gonzalez starred in basketball and football in college. He chose to play for the Chiefs when he graduated. His size, speed, and strength made him an All-Pro tight end. Gonzalez led the NFL with 102 catches in 2004.

PRIEST HOLMES   Running Back

• BORN: 10/7/1973   • PLAYED FOR TEAM: 2001 TO 2007

Priest Holmes proved that big things come in small packages. Though he stood just 5'9", he was a swift and powerful runner. Holmes led the NFL in rushing yards in 2001 and in rushing touchdowns in 2002 and 2003.

LARRY JOHNSON   Running Back

• BORN: 11/19/1979   • FIRST SEASON WITH TEAM: 2003

When Priest Holmes suffered a neck injury in 2004, Larry Johnson did a great job filling his shoes. He set a team record with 1,750 yards in 2005 and then broke his mark with 1,789 yards in 2006.

On the Sidelines

The man behind the Chiefs and their success was Lamar Hunt. He was the son of oil *tycoon* H.L. Hunt and used his family's money to *promote* sports in the United States. The American Football League was largely his idea. Hunt was beloved by fans and players. After he died in 2006, the Chiefs added a patch to their uniforms that read "L.H. AFL."

Hunt loved to hire strong and imaginative coaches. Hank Stram took the Chiefs to two Super Bowls. He was known for two new strategies. The first was to use two tight ends instead of one, which gave the Chiefs an extra blocker on the **line of scrimmage**. The second strategy was to always put a defensive player directly across from the center. This made it very hard for Kansas City's opponents to run up the middle.

Other Kansas City coaches included Marv Levy, Marty Schottenheimer, and Dick Vermeil—three of the greatest minds in NFL history. In 2006, Herm Edwards became head coach of the Chiefs. He once wrote a book called *You Play to Win the Game.*

Lamar Hunt oversees construction at Arrowhead Stadium in 1972. He was personally involved in every part of the team's business—and even mowed the grass outside the team's office when he got bored!

One Great Day

Can anyone beat the Purple People Eaters? That was the question football fans were asking before Super Bowl IV. The Minnesota Vikings were favored to beat the Chiefs by two touchdowns. The Vikings had a great defense that rarely allowed more than a touchdown a game. Their offense could also be *overpowering*. As kickoff neared, no one besides the Chiefs and their fans believed Kansas City had a chance.

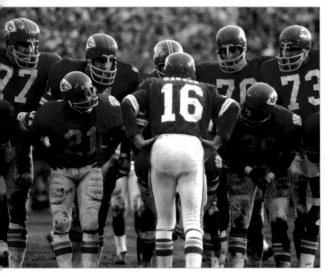

The Vikings quickly discovered that they would not be able to run against the Chiefs. Buck Buchanan and Curley Culp clogged up the middle of the line, and Kansas City's three excellent linebackers—Bobby Bell, Willie Lanier, and Jerry Lynch—tackled the Minnesota running backs when they tried to run to the outside.

The Chiefs, meanwhile, were able to move the ball close enough for Jan Stenerud to kick three field goals. With Kansas City leading

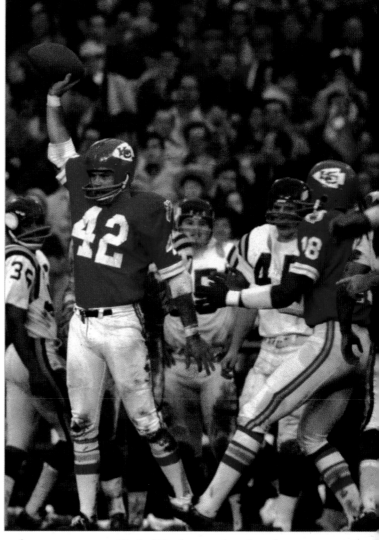

9–0, the Vikings **fumbled**, and the Chiefs recovered deep in Minnesota territory. Moments later, Mike Garrett scored a touchdown to make the score 16–0.

Minnesota finally made it into the end zone in the third quarter. The Vikings seemed to be on a roll. Len Dawson ended the ***comeback*** by leading the Chiefs right back down the field. Dawson threw a short pass to Otis Taylor, who broke two tackles and ran 41 yards for a thrilling touchdown.

Kansas City shut down the Vikings in the fourth quarter. Lanier, Johnny Robinson, and Emmitt Thomas each **intercepted** a pass. The final score was 23–7. The Chiefs proved mightier than the Purple People Eaters.

27

Legend Has It

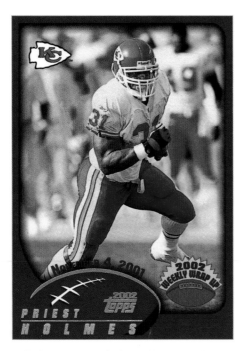

Who was the best undrafted running back in NFL history?

LEGEND HAS IT that Priest Holmes was. Football teams spend a lot of time and effort deciding which college players to pick in the draft. In 1997, no team wanted Holmes. Hundreds of players were selected, and his name was not called. Holmes tried out for the Baltimore Ravens and made the team. Four years later, he joined the Chiefs and led the NFL with 1,555 rushing yards. Only one other undrafted player, Joe Perry of the San Francisco 49ers, had ever done that before.

ABOVE: A trading card showing Priest Holmes running with the football.
RIGHT: Buck Buchanan, a star on Kansas City's great AFL teams.

Is it true that Kansas City's greatest victory did not count?

Buck
BUCHANAN
K. C. CHIEFS • DEF. TACKLE

LEGEND HAS IT that it is. After losing to the Green Bay Packers in Super Bowl I, the Chiefs were sad and *embarrassed*. All spring and summer, they had to listen to NFL players say that the AFL was no good. The Chiefs finally got a chance to prove everyone wrong in a preseason game against the NFL's Chicago Bears. Kansas City destroyed them, 66–24. Even though this game did not count in the **standings**, many Chiefs have said it was the most important win in team history.

Was the Super Bowl named after a little girl's toy?

LEGEND HAS IT that it was. When the NFL and AFL were planning to become one league, the owners got tired of saying "NFL-AFL Championship Game." One day, Kansas City owner Lamar Hunt called the game the *Super Bowl.* "I don't know where the term came from," Hunt said, "except that my daughter Sharon had a Super Ball—a little rubber ball with *phenomenal* bouncing ability … So it must have come from that."

It Really Happened

OTIS TAYLOR
CHIEFS
WIDE RECEIVER

During the 1960s, the best young football players had a choice when they were ready to join a professional league. They could play for an AFL team or an NFL team. The two leagues often fought over the top college stars. They tried to dazzle them with promises of money, cars, houses, and vacations. To impress a young player—and keep him away from the AFL—the NFL sometimes offered to treat him to a fun weekend in a fancy hotel or motel in a secret location. Who would say no to that?

In 1965, the Chiefs drafted Otis Taylor from a small college in Texas. A scout named Lloyd Wells knew Taylor and his family, and was sure he would sign with the Chiefs. Imagine his surprise when, just before the NFL draft, Taylor disappeared!

Wells searched high and low until he found Taylor. The NFL had put him up in a motel outside of Dallas. The league planned to keep him there until after its draft. Then the team that picked

Taylor could sign him to a contract. The NFL also had hired "babysitters" to make sure no one from the AFL got near Taylor while he was in his room.

Wells did not give up. Late one night, while the babysitters were standing guard in the motel lobby, he crept past the swimming pool and tapped on Taylor's back window. Wells and Taylor snuck out of the motel and took the first plane back to Kansas City. There, the Chiefs signed Taylor to a rich contract. By the time the NFL figured out

what had happened, it was too late! Taylor joined the Chiefs and became one of the greatest receivers in team history.

LEFT: Otis Taylor   **ABOVE**: Lloyd Wells did valuable work for the Chiefs. Here he tries to prevent coach Hank Stram from arguing with the referees.

Team Spirit

Sundays at Arrowhead Stadium remind many people of college football games. Fans arrive in the parking lot several hours before kickoff to meet with friends and have parties. Hours after the game is over, there are still hundreds of fans eating barbecue and talking about the Chiefs. During the games, fans sing songs and shout special chants.

For their first 25 years in Kansas City, the Chiefs had a beautiful horse named Warpaint as their *mascot*. A man named Bob Johnson wore a chief's headdress and rode Warpaint bareback. In 1989, a new mascot, K.C. Wolf, took over. During a 2007 game, he tackled a fan who had run out on the field. The fans roared their approval as K.C. showed off his bodybuilding poses.

Another favorite of the fans is the TD Pack Band. They set up behind the end zone and play music during the game. The band was started by Tony "Mr. Music" DiPardo. His daughter, Patti, took over many years ago. Mr. Music was still playing his trumpet in the band in his 90s!

Fans celebrate with Bernard Pollard after a big play in a 2007 game.

Timeline

In this timeline, each Super Bowl is listed under the year it was played. Remember that the Super Bowl is held early in the year and is actually part of the previous season. For example, Super Bowl XLII was played on February 3rd, 2008, but it was the championship of the 2007 NFL season.

1960
The team plays its first game as the Dallas Texans.

1970
The Chiefs win Super Bowl IV.

1962
The Texans win the AFL Championship, and then move to Kansas City in 1963.

1967
The Chiefs play in the first Super Bowl.

1974
Emmitt Thomas leads the NFL with 12 interceptions.

A pin worn by Chiefs fans in the 1960s.

Emmitt Thomas

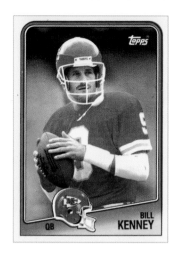

Bill
Kenney

Joe
Montana

1983
Bill Kenney leads
the AFC with 4,348
passing yards.

1993
Joe Montana leads the
Chiefs to the AFC
Championship game.

2007
Jared Allen leads the
NFL with 15.5 sacks.

1989
Christian Okoye
leads the NFL
in rushing.

1990
Derrick Thomas
leads the NFL
with 20 sacks.

2002
Dante Hall scores on a
punt and kickoff return
in the same game.

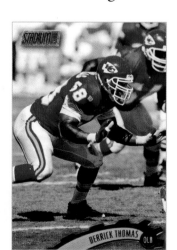

Derrick
Thomas

Dante
Hall

Fun Facts

CLEANING UP

Len Dawson hated to get his uniform dirty. His teammates nicknamed him "Ajax" after the well-known cleaning product.

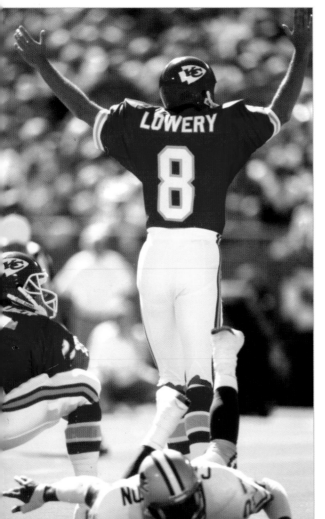

NICK OF TIME

Nick Lowery played for eight different teams and was cut 11 times before he made it with the Chiefs. He became one of the most accurate field goal kickers in history!

SECOND TO NONE

The 1969 Chiefs finished behind the Oakland Raiders in the AFL's Western Division, but they ended up winning the Super Bowl. It was the first time a second-place team won an NFL Championship.

ABOVE: Nick Lowery celebrates a field goal.
RIGHT: Joe Delaney

LIFE SAVER

In 1981, a fearless running back named Joe Delaney set a Chiefs record with 1,121 yards. During the summer of 1983, Delaney saw three little boys drowning in a pond. He did not know how to swim but dove in anyway. Delaney was able to save one of the boys before he himself drowned.

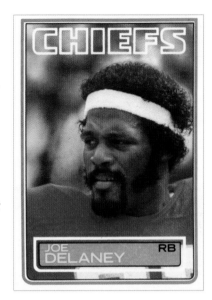

PUT ME IN, COACH

In 2004, the NFL started a Junior Player Development Program. Larry Johnson was the first to sign up and coach a middle school football team.

TOUCHDOWN CELEBRATION

In 2002, Priest Holmes broke Abner Haynes's team mark for touchdowns in a season with 21. The record had stood for 40 years. Holmes topped that mark a year later with 27 touchdowns.

BUDDE SYSTEM

From 1963 to 1986, the Chiefs had a Budde playing left guard in all but three seasons. Ed Budde was the heart of the team's offensive line in the 1960s and 1970s. His son, Brad, starred for the Chiefs in the 1980s.

Talking Football

"Tight end is one of the hardest positions to play in football. It's right up there with quarterback and cornerback. You have to have the skills of a wide receiver and the strength of an offensive lineman, and it's not easy to balance those two."

—Tony Gonzalez, on the challenges of his position

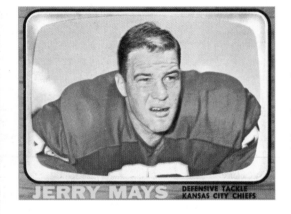

"Football can be the most miserable thing to a guy who doesn't love it, but it's the most joyous to a guy who does."

—Jerry Mays, on his love of football

"I think young people are looking for leadership. They want to know who's in charge."

—Hank Stram, on why he was a strict coach

"Confidence—it grows with victories and success."

—Jim Tyrer, on how winning improves team spirit

ABOVE: Jerry Mays
RIGHT: Marcus Allen

"When you have ambitions to play this game, you want to be one of the best ever, and you want to play so well and be so effective that you want people to remember your name 100 years from now."

—Marcus Allen, on what it takes to become a football legend

"Every time I go home to Norway, my parents ask me what I'm going to do when I grow up."

—Jan Stenerud, on playing a "kid's game" for a living

"I really like defensive players. I've never played defense so I often wonder how they think."

—Priest Holmes, on his respect for the players who try to tackle him

"Otis made my job easy. If you got the pass to Otis, you knew he'd catch it."

—Len Dawson, on his favorite receiver, Otis Taylor

For the Record

The great Texans and Chiefs teams and players have left their marks on the record books. These are the "best of the best" ...

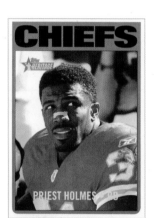

Priest Holmes

Bill Maas

CHIEFS AWARD WINNERS

WINNER	AWARD	YEAR
Abner Haynes	AFL Most Valuable Player	1960
Abner Haynes	AFL Rookie of the Year*	1960
Curtis McClinton	AFL Rookie of the Year	1962
Hank Stram	AFL Coach of the Year	1968
Len Dawson	Super Bowl MVP	1969
Bill Maas	Defensive Rookie of the Year	1984
Derrick Thomas	Defensive Rookie of the Year	1989
Barry Word	Comeback Player of the Year	1990
Dale Carter	Defensive Rookie of the Year	1992
Marcus Allen	Comeback Player of the Year	1993
Priest Holmes	Offensive Player of the Year	2002

The award given to a league's best first-year player.

Barry Word

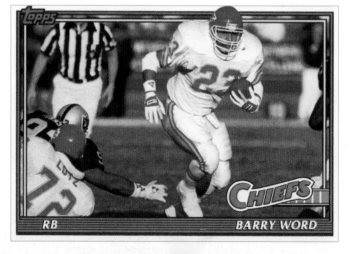

CHIEFS ACHIEVEMENTS

ACHIEVEMENT	YEAR
AFL West Champions	1962
AFL Champions	1962
AFL West Champions	1966
AFL Champions	1966
AFL Champions	1969
Super Bowl IV Champions	1969*
AFC West Champions	1971
AFC West Champions	1993
AFC West Champions	1995
AFC West Champions	1997
AFC West Champions	2003

Super Bowls are played early the following year, but the game is counted as the championship of this season.

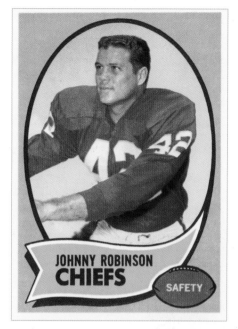

JOHNNY ROBINSON
CHIEFS
SAFETY

JAN STENERUD
CHIEFS
KICKER

TOP RIGHT: Johnny Robinson
BOTTOM RIGHT: Jan Stenerud, who starred with Robinson in the 1960s.
LEFT: Derrick Thomas

41

Pinpoints

The history of a football team is made up of many smaller stories. These stories take place all over the map—not just in the city a team calls "home." Match the pushpins on these maps to the Team Facts and you will begin to see the story of the Texans and Chiefs unfold!

TEAM FACTS

1 Kansas City, Missouri—*The team has played here since 1963.*

2 Dallas, Texas—*The team played here as the Texans from 1960 to 1962.*

3 Torrance, California—*Tony Gonzalez was born here.*

4 St. Louis, Missouri—*Trent Green was born here.*

5 Miami, Florida—*Derrick Thomas was born here.*

6 Shelby, North Carolina—*Bobby Bell was born here.*

7 Riverside, New Jersey—*Deron Cherry was born here.*

8 State College, Pennsylvania—*Larry Johnson was born here.*

9 Alliance, Ohio—*Len Dawson was born here.*

10 Gainesville, Alabama—*Buck Buchanan was born here.*

11 Fetsund, Norway—*Jan Stenerud was born here.*

12 Enugu, Nigeria—*Christian Okoye was born here.*

Bobby Bell

Play Ball

Football is a sport played by two teams on a field that is 100 yards long. The game is divided into four 15-minute quarters. Each team must have 11 players on the field at all times. The group that has the ball is called the offense. The group trying to keep the offense from moving the ball forward is called the defense.

A football game is made up of a series of "plays." Each play starts and ends with a referee's signal. A play begins when the center snaps the ball between his legs to the quarterback. The quarterback then gives the ball to a teammate, throws (or "passes") the ball to a teammate, or runs with the ball himself. The job of the defense is to tackle the player with the ball or stop the quarterback's pass. A play ends when the ball (or player holding the ball) is "down." The offense must move the ball forward at least 10 yards every four downs. If it fails to do so, the other team is given the ball. If the offense has not made 10 yards after three downs—and does not want to risk losing the ball—it can kick (or "punt") the ball to make the other team start from its own end of the field.

At each end of a football field is a goal line, which divides the field from the end zone. A team must run or pass the ball over the goal line to score a touchdown, which counts for six points. After scoring a touchdown, a team can try a short kick for one "extra point," or try again to run or pass across the goal line for two points. Teams can score three points from anywhere on the field by kicking the ball between the goal posts. This is called a field goal.

The defense can score two points if it tackles a player while he is in his own end zone. This is called a safety. The defense can also score points by taking the ball away from the offense and crossing the opposite goal line for a touchdown. The team with the most points after 60 minutes is the winner.

Football may seem like a very hard game to understand, but the more you play and watch football, the more "little things" you are likely to notice. The next time you are at a game, look for these plays:

PLAY LIST

BLITZ—A play where the defense sends extra tacklers after the quarterback. If the quarterback sees a blitz coming, he passes the ball quickly. If he does not, he can end up at the bottom of a very big pile!

DRAW—A play where the offense pretends it will pass the ball, and then gives it to a running back. If the offense can "draw" the defense to the quarterback and his receivers, the running back should have lots of room to run.

FLY PATTERN—A play where a team's fastest receiver is told to "fly" past the defensive backs for a long pass. Many long touchdowns are scored on this play.

SQUIB KICK—A play where the ball is kicked a short distance on purpose. A squib kick is used when the team kicking off does not want the other team's fastest player to catch the ball and run with it.

SWEEP—A play where the ball carrier follows a group of teammates moving sideways to "sweep" the defense out of the way. A good sweep gives the runner a chance to gain a lot of yards before he is tackled or forced out of bounds.

Glossary

AFC CHAMPIONSHIP—The game played to determine which AFC team will go to the Super Bowl.

AFC WEST—A division for teams that play in the western part of the country.

AFL CHAMPIONSHIP—The game that decided the winner of the American Football League.

ALL-AFL—An honor given to the best players at each position in the AFL.

ALL-AROUND—Good at many different parts of the game.

ALL-PRO—An honor given to the best players at their position at the end of each season.

AMERICAN FOOTBALL CONFERENCE (AFC)—One of two groups of teams that make up the NFL. The winner of the AFC plays the winner of the National Football Conference (NFC) in the Super Bowl.

AMERICAN FOOTBALL LEAGUE (AFL)—The football league that began play in 1960 and later merged with the NFL.

BLOCK—Use the body to protect the ball carrier.

DRAFT—Choose from a group of the best college players.

FREE AGENTS—Players who are allowed to sign with any team that wants them.

FUMBLED—Dropped the ball.

HALL OF FAME—The museum in Canton, Ohio, where football's greatest players are honored. A player voted into the Hall of Fame is sometimes called a "Hall of Famer."

INTERCEPTED—Caught in the air by a defensive player.

LINE OF SCRIMMAGE—The imaginary line that separates the offense and defense before each play begins.

LINEUP—The list of players on a team.

NATIONAL FOOTBALL LEAGUE (NFL)—The league that started in 1920 and is still operating today.

OVERTIME—The extra period played when a game is tied after 60 minutes.

PLAYOFFS—The games played after the season to determine which teams play in the Super Bowl.

PRO BOWL—The NFL's all-star game, played after the Super Bowl.

PROFESSIONAL—A player or team that plays a sport for money.

ROOKIE—A player in his first season.

SACKS—Tackles of the quarterback behind the line of scrimmage.

SOCCER-STYLE—Approaching the ball on an angle, instead of straight on.

STANDINGS—A list of teams, starting with the team with the best record and ending with the team with the worst record.

SUPER BOWL—The championship of football, played between the winners of the NFC and AFC.

WESTERN DIVISION—A group of teams that play in the western part of the country.

OTHER WORDS TO KNOW

ARTIFICIAL—Made by people, not nature.

CENTURY—A period of 100 years.

COMEBACK—The process of catching up from behind, or making up a large deficit.

CORE—The central part of something.

DOMINANT—Ruling or controlling.

EMBARRASSED—A feeling of dismay.

HERITAGE—Something important that is passed down through time.

MASCOT—An animal or person believed to bring a group good luck.

MODERNIZE—Bring up to date.

OVERPOWERING—Amazingly strong or forceful.

PANICKED—Got nervous.

PHENOMENAL—Amazing or incredible.

POISE—Calm and confident.

PROMOTE—Contribute to the growth of something.

RIVALS—Extremely emotional competitors.

STRATEGY—A plan or method for succeeding.

TAILBONE—The bone that protects the base of the spine.

TRADITION—A belief or custom that is handed down from generation to generation.

TYCOON—A person with great wealth and power.

Places to Go

ON THE ROAD

KANSAS CITY CHIEFS
One Arrowhead Drive
Kansas City, Missouri 64129
(816) 924-9300

THE PRO FOOTBALL HALL OF FAME
2121 George Halas Drive NW
Canton, Ohio 44708
(330) 456-8207

ON THE WEB

THE NATIONAL FOOTBALL LEAGUE   www.nfl.com
  • *Learn more about the National Football League*

THE KANSAS CITY CHIEFS   www.kcchiefs.com
  • *Learn more about the Chiefs*

THE PRO FOOTBALL HALL OF FAME   www.profootballhof.com
  • *Learn more about football's greatest players*

ON THE BOOKSHELF

To learn more about the sport of football, look for these books at your library or bookstore:

  • Fleder, Rob–Editor. *The Football Book*. New York, New York: Sports Illustrated Books, 2005.

  • Kennedy, Mike. *Football*. Danbury, Connecticut: Franklin Watts, 2003.

  • Savage, Jeff. *Play by Play Football*. Minneapolis, Minnesota: Lerner Sports, 2004.

Index

PAGE NUMBERS IN **BOLD** REFER TO ILLUSTRATIONS.

The Team

MARK STEWART has written more than 20 books on football, and over 100 sports books for kids. He grew up in New York City during the 1960s rooting for the Giants and Jets, and now takes his two daughters, Mariah and Rachel, to watch them play in their home state of New Jersey. Mark comes from a family of writers. His grandfather was Sunday Editor of *The New York Times* and his mother was Articles Editor of *The Ladies' Home Journal* and *McCall's*. Mark has profiled hundreds of athletes over the last 20 years. He has also written several books about New York and New Jersey. Mark is a graduate of Duke University, with a degree in History. He lives with his daughters and wife Sarah overlooking Sandy Hook, New Jersey.

JASON AIKENS is the Collections Curator at the Pro Football Hall of Fame. He is responsible for the preservation of the Pro Football Hall of Fame's collection of artifacts and memorabilia and obtaining new donations of memorabilia from current players and NFL teams. Jason has a Bachelor of Arts in History from Michigan State University and a Master's in History from Western Michigan University where he concentrated on sports history. Jason has been working for the Pro Football Hall of Fame since 1997; before that he was an intern at the College Football Hall of Fame. Jason's family has roots in California and has been following the St. Louis Rams since their days in Los Angeles, California. He lives with his wife Cynthia and their daughter Angelina in Canton, Ohio.